GET INTO MIXED MEDIA

GET-INTO-IT GUIDES

JANICE DYER

CRABTREE
Publishing Company
www.crabtreebooks.com

Author: Janice Dyer

Editors: Marcia Abramson, Philip Gebhardt

Photo research: Melissa McClellan

Editorial director: Kathy Middleton

Cover/Interior Design: T.J. Choleva

Production coordinator and Prepress technician: Samara Parent

Print coordinator: Margaret Amy Salter

Consultant: Trevor Hodgson, former director od The Dundas Valley School of Art in Dundas, Ontario

Developed and produced for Crabtree Publishing by BlueApple*Works* Inc.

Project Designers
Inspirational Poster, page 20 – Sarah Hodgson. Sgraffito Masterpiece, page 22 – Sarah Hodgson. Awesome Portrait – Sarah Hodgson. 3-D Adventure, page 26 – Jane Yates. Abstract Paint Art, page 28 – Jane Yates.

Photographs

Shutterstock.com: © Zadorozhnyi Viktor (cover top banner); © Rudchenko Liliia (top far right); © kristala (cover center); © donatas1205 (cover far left); © Opas Chotiphan-tawanon (TOC); © Mostovyi Sergii Igorevich (p. 5 left); © Gilmanshin (p. 6 top left); © Aigars Reinholds (p. 6 top middle); © Prajak Poonyawatpornkul (p. 6 top right); © JIPEN (p. 6 left 2cd from top); © Stephanie Zieber (p. 6 right 2cd from top); © GUNDAM_Ai (p. 6 left 3rd from top); © imagedb.com (p. 6 bottom left); © Imageman (p. 6 bottom right); © aekikuis (p. 7 top); © Will Thomass (p. 8 top right); © Happy Stock Photo (p. 8 middle right); © ilolab (p. 10 top left); © Katsiaryna Maksimovich (p. 10 top right); © dona-tas1205 (p. 10 bottom left); © DeepGreen (p. 10 bottom right); © valkoinen (p. 11 bottom left); © Lipskiy (p. 11 bottom middle); © Bryan Solomon (p. 11 bottom right); © Taiga (p. 12 middle right); Marina Zakharova (p. 14 top right); © eakkachai halang (p. 19 top left); © Nuttapong (p. 15 middle bottom); © Pabkov (p. 19 top middle); © paranut (p. 19 top right); © Laboko (p. 20–21 top); © Volga (p. 20 middle right); © NY-P (p. 21 top left); © Mostovyi Sergii Igorevich (p. 24–25 top); © Thirteen (p. 26–27 top); © NataPro (p. 28–29 top); Alamy: © Josse Christophel/Alamy Stock Photo (p. 5 right); © Alfonso Vicente/Alamy Stock Photo (p. 29 top right);Courtesy of Nina Jain (p. 29 bottom right); © Austen Photography (front cover, title page,TOC, p. 4 left, p. 8 bottom, p. 9, 10, 11, 12, 13, 14, 15, 16, 17, 18, 19, 21 right, 25 right, 26, 27, 28, 29, 31, 32, back cover); © Molly Klager (p. 4 right, 20 bottom right, 29 bottom left, 30; © Sarah Hodgson (p. 20, 21, 22, 23, 24, 25, back cover bottom right

Library and Archives Canada Cataloguing in Publication

Dyer, Janice, author
    Get into mixed media / Janice Dyer.

(Get-into-it guides)
Includes index.
Issued in print and electronic formats.
ISBN 978-0-7787-3402-4 (hardcover).—
ISBN 978-0-7787-3406-2 (softcover).--
ISBN 978-1-4271-1915-5 (HTML)

    1. Mixed media (Art)--Juvenile literature. 2. Mixed media (Art)--
Technique--Juvenile literature. 3. Handicraft--Juvenile literature.
I. Title.

TT160.D94 2017   j745.5   C2016-907386-6
                                        C2016-907387-4

Library of Congress Cataloging-in-Publication Data

Names: Dyer, Janice, author.
Title: Get into mixed media / Janice Dyer.
Description: New York : Crabtree Publishing Company, 2017. | Series: Get-Into-It Guides | Includes index.
Identifiers: LCCN 2017000387 (print) | LCCN 2017001777 (ebook) | ISBN 9780778734024 (reinforced library binding : alk. paper) | ISBN 9780778734062 (pbk. : alk. paper) | ISBN 9781427119155 (Electronic HTML)
Subjects: LCSH: Mixed media (Art)--Technique--Juvenile literature.
Classification: LCC TT160 .D94 2017 (print) | LCC TT160 (ebook) | DDC 745.5--dc23
LC record available at https://lccn.loc.gov/2017000387

Crabtree Publishing Company
www.crabtreebooks.com   1-800-387-7650

Printed in Canada/032017/BF20170111

Published in Canada
Crabtree Publishing
616 Welland Ave.
St. Catharines, Ontario
L2M 5V6

Published in the United States
Crabtree Publishing
PMB 59051
350 Fifth Avenue, 59th Floor
New York, New York 10118

Published in the United Kingdom
Crabtree Publishing
Maritime House
Basin Road North, Hove
BN41 1WR

Published in Australia
Crabtree Publishing
3 Charles Street
Coburg North
VIC, 3058

CONTENTS

MIXED MEDIA ART

Imagine creating artwork using different materials and different **techniques**. That's what mixed media art is all about! For example, you could combine paint, ink, and a technique called **collage** to create a portrait, or use clay, stamps, and **found objects** to create a model or **diorama**. Artists use color, **texture**, lines, shapes, space, and **dimension** to create their masterpieces.

The nice thing about creating mixed media art is that you don't need to be an artist or to be able to draw to create something special. To get started, you just need to be able to use a pencil, scissors, and glue—that's it! Another great thing about creating mixed media projects is that you can use all kinds of materials in your art, from buttons, beads, and glue to paint, paper, photos, stamps, stickers, and yarn. The possibilities are endless.

You can have a lot of fun creating art using mixed media. Try using the techniques in this book to make a mixed media work of art!

THE HISTORY OF MIXED MEDIA ART

People began using the term "mixed media" in the early 1990s. However, the idea of mixed media art has been around for centuries. For instance, artists in the Byzantine Empire (330 to 1453 B.C.E.) added **gold leaf** to their paintings, **mosaics**, and texts. Gold leaf is gold that has been hammered into a very thin sheet and then used to cover statues, picture frames, or other parts of a piece of art. In ancient Egypt, artists used gold leaf on their oil paintings to make the sky look shiny.

HOW TO USE THIS BOOK

The projects in this book are meant to inspire you to create your own mixed media art. You can follow the steps provided or use your imagination to add your own ideas to a project.

Did You Know?

Many famous artists from history used mixed media to create their artwork. Experts consider Pablo Picasso's piece of art called Still Life with Chair Caning as the first modern mixed media artwork. Picasso used paint, cloth, and rope to create a 3-D masterpiece using a new technique called collage.

The term collage was coined by Pablo Picasso and his colleague artist Georges Braque in the early 20th century.

Creative Huddle

Pablo Picasso said: "All children are artists. The problem is how to remain an artist once he [she] grows up." What do you think Picasso meant by this?

IT'S ALL ABOUT THE LAYERS

Artists who work in mixed media use layers of different materials to create their art. They might glue **found objects**, like feathers, sticks, or stones, to a painting done on canvas. Others might choose to add layers of different colors of paper or photographs to create a **3-dimensional (3-D)** effect. You can also use mixed media techniques to decorate books or boxes or to create greeting cards and gift tags.

Mixed media projects are a great way to recycle things that would normally go in the garbage. Start collecting boxes, paper, buttons, and other bits and pieces to use in your next masterpiece.

5

MATERIALS AND COLORS TO FIT YOUR STYLE

You can make many of the mixed media art projects in this book with recycled materials found around the house. Collect scraps of fabric and paper, newspapers, egg cartons, mailing tubes, magazines, toilet paper and paper towel rolls, and stickers. You might also want to use things such as buttons, clay, yarn, beads, and string.

You can also use different kinds of art supplies such as paint, pencils, markers, clay, crayons, pastels, charcoal, ink, glue, and scissors!

watercolor paint and brushes

old magazines

acrylic paint and brushes

How to Choose?

It can feel overwhelming when you are starting a project. What materials should you use? The possibilities seem endless!

Start by **brainstorming** a list of materials that you know will be easy to find around your home or neighborhood, or that you can borrow from a friend.

sponges and sponge brushes

○ Decide which materials are the best fit for what you are planning to create.

○ Gather all your materials, so they are handy.

○ Start creating!

Just use your imagination!

oil pastels

ink pad   *markers*

WORKING WITH COLORS

Artists use the color wheel as a tool to help them mix colors. The wheel shows how colors are related to each other and how they can be combined to create new colors. It also shows which colors will look best with other colors.

The color wheel is divided into three types of colors: primary, secondary, and tertiary. The **primary colors** are red, blue, and yellow. These three colors cannot be made from mixing other colors together, so they are called primary, which means "first." The **secondary colors** are green, orange, and violet or purple. These colors are made by mixing two primary colors. For example, if you mix red and yellow, you get orange. **Tertiary**, which means "third," are colors made by mixing primary and secondary colors next to each other on the wheel.

COMPLEMENTARY COLORS

When you are choosing colors for your art project, remember that colors from opposite sides of the wheel **complement** or balance each other. For example, red and green, yellow and violet, and blue and orange are sets of complementary colors. Using these types of colors will make your project stand out.

USING THE RIGHT COLORS

The color wheel can also be divided into warm and cool colors. Warm colors such as red, yellow, and orange appear bright, vivid, and energetic. Cool colors such as blue, violet, and green are more calming, and tend to create a soothing impression. Think about the impression you want to show through your art and pick the right colors to create the proper mood.

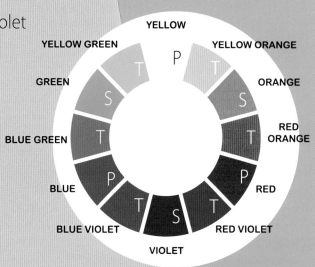

P – *Primary colors*
S – *Secondary colors*
T – *Tertiary colors*

Yellow and blue are two neighboring primary colors. Mixing them together will create the green secondary color.

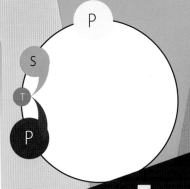

Green and blue are two neighboring primary and secondary colors. Mixing them together will create the blue-green tertiary color.

BACKGROUND SURFACES

Mixed media artists layer materials to create an image with texture. But before you can start creating your work, you need to choose a background.

You can use a variety of different materials for the background of your mixed media project. Start with any of these examples: canvas, watercolor paper, fabric, wood, cardboard, or a cereal or shoe box.

STURDY BACKGROUNDS

If you are creating a collage or multi-layered piece of art, it is important to have a sturdy background. You can use things such as canvas, cardboard, wood, or fabric to give you a solid foundation for your art. Make sure the background is strong enough to support what you are planning to do. For instance, if you are using layers of paint, cardboard will work well. If you are using wire, stones, and other heavy items, you might want to use a piece of wood for your background.

WORKING WITH CANVAS

You can buy ready-made stretched canvas or canvas boards in an art supply store to use for your art. If you want to add some originality, make your own canvas using burlap, fabric, or any rough-textured material that will work well with your art ideas. Follow the instructions below to prepare a burlap canvas background for your project.

WHAT YOU WILL NEED
- ✔ any sturdy box such as a pizza or shoe box
- ✔ brush
- ✔ glue
- ✔ burlap
- ✔ gesso (see page 9)

Paint the back and sides of the box with white paint. Let the paint dry.

Cut a piece of burlap or other fabric large enough to cover the box and wrap around the sides.

WATERCOLOR PAPER AND MIXED MEDIA PAPER

If you are using watercolors, you need to make sure to use the right type of paper. The kind of paper you choose will affect the style of your final painting, and how long the painting lasts. The three main types of paper are hot-pressed paper, cold-pressed paper, and rough paper. Think about what your artwork will include, then choose the type of paper that will work best.

HOT-PRESSED PAPER

This paper is smooth and is great for mixed-media projects. You might want to use this type of paper if you are using watercolor paints and other media, such as ink and graphite. These materials will slide smoothly over hot-pressed paper.

COLD-PRESSED PAPER

This paper is rougher than hot-pressed paper. Many artists like using this type of paper because of its texture. The paint looks a little rough because it settles on only some of the paper, leaving blank spots where there are indentations.

ROUGH PAPER

This paper has a lot of texture to it. It is harder to paint details on this type of paper, but the texture gives your artwork a lot of character. It is fun to use this type of paper because you are never sure what the results will look like!

USING GESSO

Gesso is like thin white acrylic paint. It is an important art supply because it dries hard. If you put it on fabric, it makes the surface stiff. Gesso prepares your canvas, making it ready for painting. If you don't use gesso, the paint will soak into the canvas. You can use gesso on nearly any surface. Once it dries, you can paint the surface with acrylic paint.

Wrap the burlap around the box. Glue the edges to the inside edges of the box.

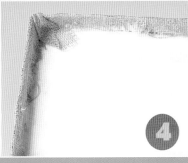

Tuck the corners in as shown and glue them in place. (Use a low-temperature glue gun if necessary.)

Flip your canvas over.

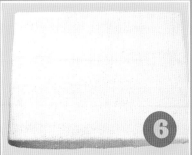

Cover the canvas with gesso.

PAINTING STYLES

PICK YOUR PAINTING TECHNIQUES

The painting techniques you use will affect how your final project looks. By combining wet and dry paint, wet and wet paint, different types of paint, different thicknesses of paint, different types of brush strokes, and different styles of painting, you can create a variety of colors, textures, and effects.

WET ON WET

Dilute ink or watercolor paint with water to create a **wash**. You can experiment with different amounts of water. **Saturate** the entire page with the wash first, then apply other colors of paint while the page is still wet.

Wet the paper so it is saturated but not so much that water is lying on top. Stroke a brush filled with blue watercolor across the paper until it is covered.

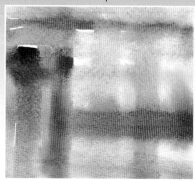

When using different colors on wet paper, the colors will blend together.

Try painting shapes on wet paper with a wet brush.

WET ON DRY

Allow the first layer of paint to dry, then paint or draw over it with a different color or material.

Paint a blue background on dry paper.

If the other colors are dry, they won't mix together when you paint over them.

With dry paper you can paint with much more detail.

IMPASTO

Use thick paint to create a 3-D image. You can use a brush or an art tool called a palette knife to apply the paint.

Apply some acrylic paint directly to your background surface.

Spread the paint around with a palette knife or brush.

You can add texture to the thick paint with a plastic fork.

Add a **gel medium** to acrylic paints to change the thickness of the paint and create different effects.

SGRAFFITO

Create one layer of oil pastels then add a layer of black tempera paint. Once the layers have dried, use a sharp pointed object to scratch through the tempera layer until the color you want shows through.

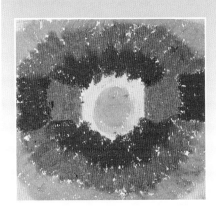

Cover the background surface with oil pastels.

Cover the pastel with a layer of black tempera or poster paint. Leave it to dry.

Scratch shapes and lines iinto the black paint to reveal the colors underneath.

You can draw with anything pointed—a wooden skewer, nail, or the pointed end of a paintbrush.

Tip

Many non-English words are used in art. Sgraffito is the Italian word for scratched. Impasto is the Italian word for paste or mixture.

SECTION PAINTING

Create a design on the surface using painter's tape. With a brush or sponge, cover the open sections in paint. When dry, remove the tape.

Place strips of tape over the background surface. Leave the edges, to make it easier to remove the tape.

Fill in each section created using the tape with paint.

Carefully pull the tape off the surface.

SPONGE-DAB PAINTING

Apply two or more colors of paint. Use a damp or dry sponge to dab the colors together.

Cover the background surface with one color.

Start sponging using another color.

Add some white to help blend the two colors. Keep adding until you are happy with your background pattern.

DRIPPED PAINTING

Work with thicker paint that is still runny. Tip a container of paint onto the background in different directions to make a design.

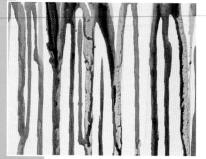

Hold the surface upright and drip paint down the background.

Drip drops of paint from a container.

Make a large puddle of paint and tip the surface in different directions so the paint drips down.

12

TEXTURE PAINTING

Mix glue and water together as shown on page 31. Glue tissue paper to the surface, creating the texture you want. When it is dry, paint over the tissue.

First crumple the tissue paper. Cover the background surface with the thinned glue.

Lay the tissue paper over the glue. carefully press down and apply another layer of the thinned glue.

When dry, you can paint over the tissue paper with another color.

TRANSFER PAINTING

Transfer a photocopy or laser-printed image to a canvas to create a great mixed media effect.

Apply a layer of gel medium to a painted canvas. Place a photocopied image face down on the wet gel and smooth out all the air bubbles. Leave it to dry.

Wet a sponge and use it to soak the image. Then rub away the paper with your fingers.

The ink from the image will have transferred to the canvas. Finish it by adding some paint to the edges of the canvas.

SPLATTER PAINTING

Cover the paintbrush bristles with paint. Gently tap the paintbrush with a second brush held in your opposite hand to splatter the paint.

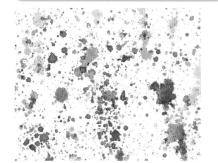

Gently tapping the brush makes tiny dots of splatter. Flick the brush to create bigger drops.

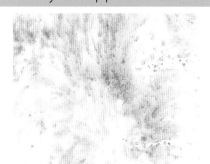

Splatter painting on wet paper using watercolors gives a blurred effect.

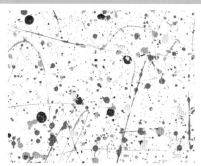

You can splatter with acryclic paint, too. Just add a little water to the paint.

13

Collage involves using glue, paper, ribbons, photographs, and other materials to create an image. You can create a simple collage using only glue and paper.

paper for collage using watercolors. Draw the letter or image on the painting and cut it out.

CUT

❶ Start by cutting out images from old magazines or tearing pieces of tissue paper into the shape you want.

GLUE

❷ Dilute craft glue with a little bit of water. Use a paintbrush to spread glue onto a small part of your background. Press the paper into the glue. Repeat until you have covered the area.

SEAL

❸ When you are finished gluing, cover the paper with a thin layer of glue to seal the paper.

CREATING A SIMPLE COLLAGE WITH WORDS

Cut sections of words to make a background.

Glue to your background surface. Leave it to dry.

Paint a light wash of watercolor over the background.

Cut out words and letters from old newspapers, magazines, or books.

❺ Arrange them in a pleasing design then transfer them to your background and glue them in place.

Prepare a background surface. This one is covered with tissue paper and edged with paint.

Draw or trace a shape on a piece of heavy paper. Cut out small pieces of specific colors from a magazine.

Cut out the shape. Glue the pieces to it until the entire shape is covered. Trim the edges. Glue your shape to the background.

Glue the shapes face down onto magazine pieces. Cut the shapes out.

Prepare a background surface. This one is painted with watercolor paint.

Draw or trace shapes on a piece of heavy paper. Cut the shapes out. You can use your own shapes, or follow the pattern on page 32 for this particular art.

Glue the shapes onto the background, magazine-side up. Be careful to coat only the figure with glue, not the background.

Making 3-D art with found objects is called **assemblage**. The choice of materials you can use to create an assemblage piece of art is endless: string, nails, buttons, shells, fabric, photos, toys, leaves, flowers, and so much more. You can make an assemblage sculpture or a collage with your items.

IDEAS FOR ASSEMBLAGE ART

Glue elements of nature such as seeds and stems to your background. Add another layer of glue on top.

Glue leaves to your art board. Cover them with another layer of glue.

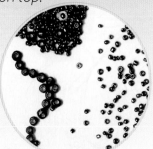

Glue beads to your background surface.

Glue yarn or twine to your art board.

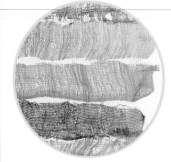

Glue fabric to your art board.

Glue buttons in a pattern to your background.

TIN CAN ASSEMBLAGE PROJECT

1

Find some items that you would like to combine together.

2

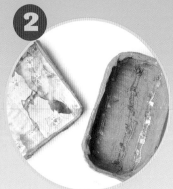

Glue tissue paper, wrapping paper, or fabric to a tin can.

3

Glue your items from step 1 to the tin can. Glue a piece of cardboard to the back of some items to make them stand out from the background to create a 3-D effect.

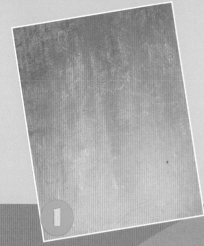

1

Paint a background on your cardboard.

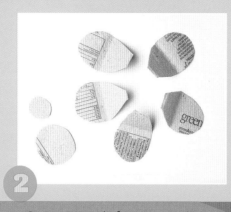

2

Cut out petals from an egg carton or cardboard. Cut out two circles for a flower center.

3

Cover the egg carton petals and one circle with paper strips and paper mache mixture. (See page 30 for paper mache instructions.) Add sequins or beads to the flower center. Leave it to dry.

4

Cut some strips of cardboard, and paint them green to use as grass.

5

Glue a piece of twine to the board for a stem. Glue the grass on top of the twine at the bottom. Glue the plain egg carton circle at the top of the twine.

6

Glue the petals to the plain circle. Glue the decorated center on top. Glue yarn around the outside as a frame.

STAMP IT - ROLL IT

Stencils are a great way to add a unique image to your artwork without having to do the drawing yourself. You can make your own stencils by cutting out shapes from a photo or picture. You can also use paper doilies or lace as stencils, or buy stencils from a craft store.

Stamping is another way to add different images, textures, and interest to your mixed media art. You can buy rubber or foam stamps from a craft store or make your own using found objects, such as the bottom of a bottle, the lid of a jar, or bubble wrap.

WORKING WITH STENCILS

Using stencils will help add visual interest to your mixed-media artwork. Stencils make it easy to add shapes and repeating patterns. You can even layer stencils to make your art look even more interesting!

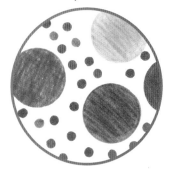

Make your own stencil by punching holes in a piece of cardboard.

Purchased stencils come in all kinds of patterns and images.

Purchase a letter stencil to add words or letters to your art.

WORKING WITH STAMPS

Stamps can be used with ink, markers, or paint. They are a great way to create patterns for an interesting background. They can add texture and visual interest.

You can purchase rubber shape or word stamps.

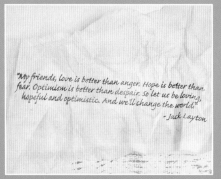

Rubber stamps with quotes are great to add to collages. Stamp it, paint it with light brown watercolor paint, then crinkle it.

CREATING SIMPLE ROLLERS

Making patterns using stamp rollers is a fun mixed-media technique. You can buy one or make your own using a paper towell roll, a small rolling pin, or a lint roller as the base. The stamp portion is attached to the roller. Apply paint with a brush to the stamp. Then roll the stamp on the surface of your choice.

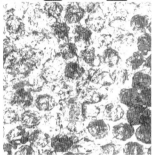
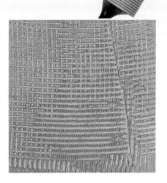
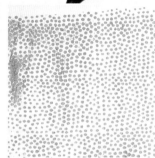

Make a simple roller stamp with twine.

Attach bubble wrap to a roller.

Tape corrugated cardboard around a roller.

Tape patterned Styrofoam around a roller.

CREATING SIMPLE STAMPS

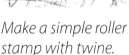

Create a foam stamp by sticking foam stickers to a base such as a piece of foam.

Create simple stamps such as pencil erasers, rectangle erasers, and plastic lids to create great patterns.

Creative Huddle

Keep a notebook and pen handy so you can record your ideas for art projects. Ideas might come to you while you are listening to music, walking, playing in the park, or relaxing after a busy day.

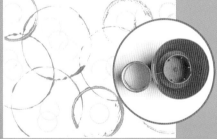

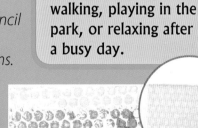
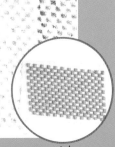

Make a shape out of Plasticine to create a stamp.

Make a texture stamp with a piece of textured shelf liner.

Bubble wrap works great, too.

19

INSPIRATIONAL POSTER

Many people like to read and display quotes to motivate themselves to do better and to help them appreciate life. This project will show you how to create your own mixed media **inspirational** poster using collage, stamping, and stencil techniques.

YOU WILL NEED:
- ✔ cardboard
- ✔ watercolors
- ✔ printing ink
  or acrylic paint
- ✔ paintbrushes
- ✔ old magazines
- ✔ Styrofoam container
- ✔ pencil
- ✔ scissors
- ✔ glue
- ✔ paper towels
- ✔ stencils and marker
  (optional)

1 *Paint the board white.*

2 *Using watercolors, paint a variety of colors on the board.*

3 *Using a dry paper towel, dab the wet watercolors to create a texture.*

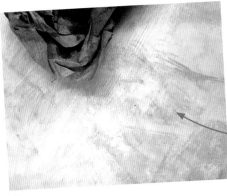

4 *Find an inspirational saying and cut the appropriate letters from old magazines or print them from your computer. The final image will be more interesting if you use a variety of styles of letters.*

5 *Place the letters where you would like them and glue them in place.*

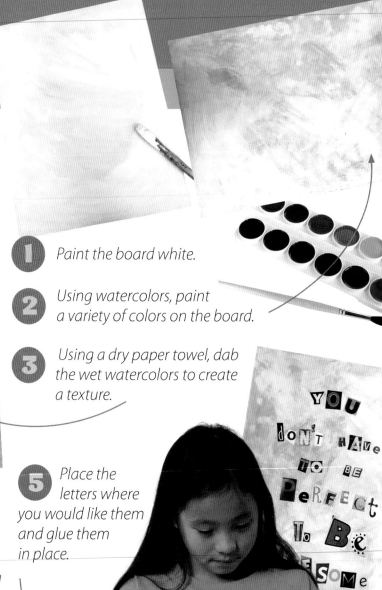

Creative Huddle

What inspires you? Think about what motivates you to do better. Do some research to find a quote that inspires you.

6 Using an old Styrofoam plate or take-out container, cut out 2 small squares.

7 Using a sharp pencil, draw a pattern on the squares.

8 Using either block printing ink or acrylic paint, paint your squares with a roller or brush.

9 Use the squares to stamp paint designs around the border of your poster. Put new paint or ink on your square each time you use it.

10 Add additional elements with stencils and markers.

SGRAFFITO MASTERPIECE

In this project, you will use sgraffito, or scratching, to create a masterpiece. By scratching into the top layer of the paint, you will reveal the colors and textures that are underneath.

YOU WILL NEED:

- gesso white
- acryclic paint
- oil pastels
- black tempera or poster paint
- cardboard or masonite
- paint brushes
- nail or wooden skewer

1 Paint a cross from corner to corner on the back of the board. This helps stop the board from warping.

2 Cover the board with gesso or white latex paint. Let the paint dry.

3 Use a ruler to draw a line for a frame pattern around your artwork, if you like.

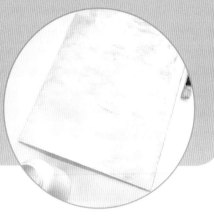

4 Using oil pastels, color a design on the white board. This can be an abstract design or a design with more of a plan (for example use greens at the bottom for grass and blues at the top for sky). You can also color a border.

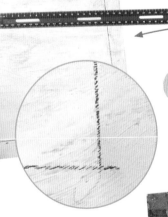

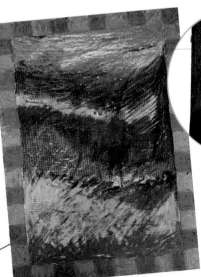

5 After you have colored everything, paint over the pastel design with black tempera or poster paint. Let the paint dry.

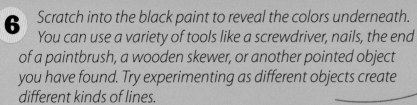

6 Scratch into the black paint to reveal the colors underneath. You can use a variety of tools like a screwdriver, nails, the end of a paintbrush, a wooden skewer, or another pointed object you have found. Try experimenting as different objects create different kinds of lines.

7 Try different styles of lines such as curves, spirals, zigzags, or **cross-hatching**.

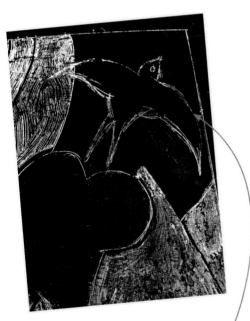

8 To draw objects such as birds or trees, scratch out the outline first, and then fill the outlined shape with decorative lines.

TIP

If you want to redo a section of the painting, paint over what you have scratched with more black paint. Leave it to dry and redo that section.

AWESOME PORTRAIT

A portrait is an image of a person. You can choose to create a portrait of yourself, your parents, your brother or sister, a friend, or even your pet. For this project, you will use collage techniques to create a portrait that shows the individual's personality and mood.

YOU WILL NEED:

- ✔ canvas board
- ✔ pencil
- ✔ acrylic paint
- ✔ brush
- ✔ glue
- ✔ scissors
- ✔ old magazines or pictures from the Internet
- ✔ colored or patterned paper, such as scrapbooking paper, wallpaper, etc.

1 *Collect a variety of materials to help you create this collage. This can include, magazines, wallpaper, colored paper, scrapbooking papers, computer printouts, paint, and pencil crayons.*

2 *Using a pencil, draw the outline of your portrait on a canvas board. Keep the shapes simple.*

3 *Find a variety of images of hair from magazines or the Internet. Cut pieces of hair from the images. Use different shades of hair because this will give your hair depth when you add it to your portrait.*

4 *Using glue, attach your hair to the canvas.*

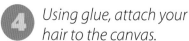

Creative Huddle

Before you start, think about the subject of your portrait. What do you want the audience to feel or think of when they look at your finished piece of art? What techniques can you use to make sure that message comes across?

5 Use some of the hair pieces to cut eyebrows for your portrait.

6 Find eyes and lips in magazines or on the Internet and print them out. If you have a black and white printer, use pencil crayons to color your eyes and lips. Glue the completed eyes and lips to your portrait. If you want to, you can also add ears.

7 Make the color you want for the skin tone by mixing different acrylic paints and a little water. Paint in the areas of the skin, including the face and the neck.

8 Use colored or patterned paper to create a shirt or dress.

9 You can also use colored or patterned paper to fill in the background. Use any shape you wish. Or, if you like, you can paint in the background. Or use both!

10 When you have completed your portrait, coat it with acrylic medium, which can help preserve the picture and give it an even look all over.

25

3-D ADVENTURE

A 3-D mixed media project is a great way to use found objects to tell a story.
You will use objects and the assemblage technique for this project.
Let your imagination run wild as you create a 3-D adventure!

YOU WILL NEED:

✔ collection of hardware bits
✔ cardboard, art board, or masonite
✔ paint and brushes
✔ bubble wrap
✔ glue (depending on the weight of the objects, you may need low-temperature hot glue)

1 Organize your collection of hardware bits and pieces. Lay them out on a piece of cardboard the same size as your art board.

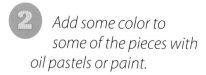

2 Add some color to some of the pieces with oil pastels or paint.

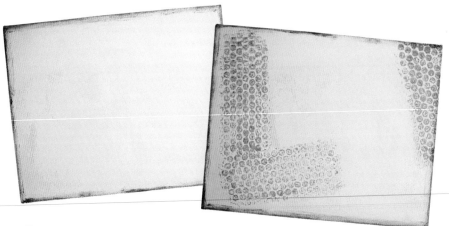

3 Create your background. Use two colors. Cover the board with one color. While still wet, blend in a lighter color. Using a sponge or ball of paper towel, add a darker color to the edge of the board.

4 Add a pattern by pressing down on bubble wrap covered in paint. Make several impressions without adding more paint to the bubble wrap. This will create variations in the pattern.

5 Glue all the pieces to the board. If layering, glue the bottom pieces first such as the legs and arms in the example.

6 Draw faces and other shapes on watercolor paper. Draw facial features with markers or oil pastels. Paint the background.

7 Glue your shapes to the hardware pieces.

DECORATING A GLASS BOTTLE INTO A VASE

1 Cut strips of tissue paper. The strips need to be a little longer than the bottle.

2 Brush paper mache glue (see page 31) onto the bottle. Place strips of tissue paper around the bottle vertically. Continue adding strips to the bottle until it is completely covered.

3 Add colored string or ribbons around the bottle opening.

4 Tear a picture from wrapping paper or a magazine and glue it to the front.

ABSTRACT PAINT ART

Abstract art uses shapes, color, lines, and form to create an image that might not look like anything from real life. Abstract artists paint what they feel. They use different colors and techniques to show their emotions. In this project, you will use a variety of painting styles to create an abstract mixed media piece of art.

YOU WILL NEED:
- ✔ stretched canvas
- ✔ painter's tape
- ✔ acrylic paint
- ✔ watercolor paint
- ✔ oil pastel
- ✔ tissue paper
- ✔ salt
- ✔ paper towel
- ✔ plastic wrap

Paint area

Protective strips of tape

Painted area

New protective strip

New paint area

1 *Apply tape to one end of the canvas. Paint the untaped portion of the canvas. Let it dry, then remove the tape.*

2 *Apply a new strip of tape to protect part of the painted area. Now, paint the unpainted area. Let it dry, then remove the tape.*

4 *Tear narrow strips of painter's tape and add them to the canvas extending out from the circle.*

3 *Draw an arc in one corner of the canvas using an oil pastel.*

5 *Add a watercolor wash to the circle. While the paint is still wet, sprinkle salt over the paint to create a texture.*

Creative Huddle

Tape is a great way to make many different mixed media effects. Think of other ways to use tape in your art.

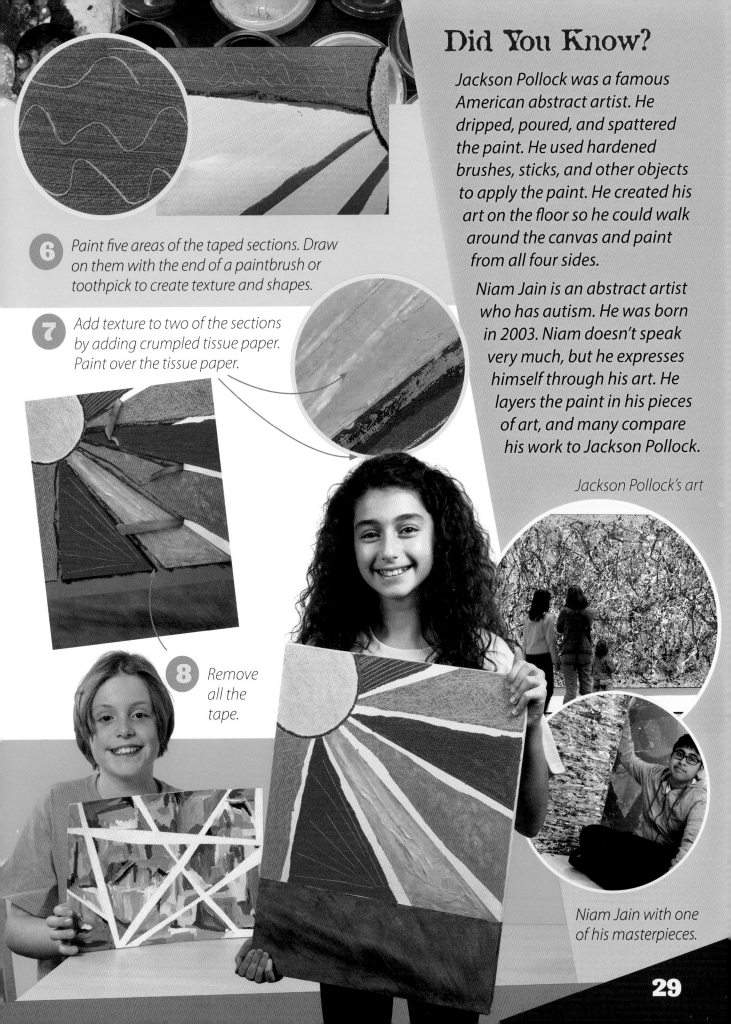

6 Paint five areas of the taped sections. Draw on them with the end of a paintbrush or toothpick to create texture and shapes.

7 Add texture to two of the sections by adding crumpled tissue paper. Paint over the tissue paper.

8 Remove all the tape.

LEARNING MORE

Books

101 Mixed Media Techniques
by Isaac Anderson, Cherril Doty, Samantha Kira Harding, Jennifer McCully, Suzette Rosenthal, and Linda Roberson Womack. Walter Foster Publishing, 2014.

ARTrageous! by Jennifer McCully. Walter Foster Publishing, 2015.

Paint Lab for Kids: 52 Create Adventures in Painting and Mixed Media for Budding Artists of all Ages by Stephanie Corfee. Quarry Publishing Group, 2015.

Websites

Happy Family Art
www.happyfamilyart.com/art-lessons/mixed-media-art-lessons
Ideas for a variety of mixed media projects using different techniques.

Mixed Media Art Projects
www.createmixedmedia.com/make
Tutorials for creating mixed media art projects.

Meet Artist Niam Jain
http://niamjain.com/about-niam-jain/
Get inspired by the art of young abstract artist Niam Jain, who has autism.

PAPER MACHE TECHNIQUE

MOLD

Before you start applying paper strips, prepare your mold and shapes for the bases. You can create forms from crumpled newspapers and cardboard products, bowls or plates, or balloons. Paper towel rolls and pipe cleaners work well, too. Balloons are great for round shapes because they will tear away from your dried paper mache easily when burst. When using bowls or plates, cover them with a thin layer of vaseline first to stop the paper mache from sticking to them.

GLUE

Once your molds are ready, it is time to apply the paper strips. Cover the strips of paper with glue on both sides with a paintbrush. Then place your strips one at a time over the mold, smoothing the strips to remove any air bubbles. Cover the mold with two or three layers at a time. If you put too many layers on at once, it will take too long to dry. Build up the layers until you have the thickness you want.

PAINT

When completely dry, cover your creation with two coats of paint to seal it. You can use any type of paint, but the most popular paint is water-based acrylic. It is easy to use, and also quick to dry.

GLOSSARY

3-dimensional (3-D) Something that has height, width, and depth

assemblage A 3-D work of art made using found objects

brainstorm To think about a plan or a solution

collage Art made by gluing different materials onto a background

complement To boost or improve something else

cross-hatching Marks with two series of parallel lines that cross each other

dilute To make a liquid thinner using water

dimension The length, breadth, depth, or height

found objects Objects from nature or around the house that can be used in artwork, such as feathers, sticks, leaves

gel medium A thick gel that can be mixed with acrylic paints to create interesting texture effects and glossy appearance

gold leaf Gold hammered into thin sheets that can be shaped and used in artwork

inspirational Making you feel full of hope or encouraged

mosaic A pattern or picture made by arranging small pieces of colored stone, tile, or glass

primary colors In painting, any of the three colors (red, yellow, and blue) that cannot be made by mixing other colors together

saturate Soak thoroughly

secondary colors Colors made by mixing two primary colors

techniques Methods

tertiary colors Colors made by mixing primary and secondary colors

texture The feel or look of a surface

wash A thin coat of paint or ink diluted with water

PAPER MACHE GLUE

YOU WILL NEED:

- ✔ large mixing bowl (8 cup or 1.9 L)
- ✔ newspaper
- ✔ 1 cup (250 mL) flour or glue
- ✔ 3 tablespoons (45 mL) salt
- ✔ 2 cups (500 mL) water
- ✔ measuring cup
- ✔ spoon

Paper Mache Glue - Made with Flour

Add flour and salt to a bowl and add water slowly, mixing with a spoon. Continue to add water until your paste is like a thin pancake batter, smooth with no lumps.

Paper Mache Glue - Made with Glue

Add 1 cup (250 mL) white glue and 2 cups (500 mL) water to a bowl. Mix together with a spoon until the mixture is well-blended.

INDEX

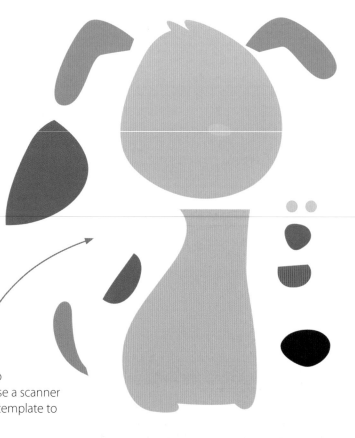

Pattern for the collage art on page 15

Note: This template is reduced to 50 percent of the original size. Use a scanner or a photocopier to enlarge the template to 200 percent.